ANTIQUE FURNITURE
EXPLAINED
AND ILLUSTRATED
(1500—1901)

ANTIQUE FURNITURE

Explained and Illustrated

(1500—1901)

by

K. W. M. Bowers
F.S.A.(Scot.), F.R.S.A.

Gramercy Publishing Company
New York

CONTENTS

ILLUSTRATIONS

INTRODUCTION

For purposes of convenient classification the history
of English furniture, up to 1805, has been divided
into three sections, each named after the wood used
predominantly for the manufacture of products
during the period concerned—the Age of Oak
(1500–1660), the Age of Walnut (1660–1720) and
the Age of Mahogany (1720–1805). The appella-
tions are not of literal accuracy—for instance,
woods other than oak were of course used during
the years between 1500 and 1660, and oak itself has
continued to be used as one of the staple materials
of the furniture trade throughout succeeding centuries. The ages thus named are, however, a satisfactory guide to the general flavour of the three
periods.

The latter few years of the Age of Mahogany are
sometimes known as the Age of Satinwood, owing
to the introduction, at that time, of the hitherto unexploited timber. The Mahogany Period is
followed by the Regency (1805–1830) and the Victorian Era (1830–1901).

In a condensed history, concentration must be
directed upon general trends in design and construction, but the many variations on every fresh

innovation, which were made throughout the country should not be neglected. Many examples encountered today are likely to be 'country pieces', therefore some confusion in period identification is possible—especially as designs originating in earlier periods persisted for many years in the more remote parts. For instance, chests of the archaic construction usually associated with the fifteenth and sixteenth centuries, were still being made in many rural districts of the British Isles well into the 1650s. Standards of craftsmanship cannot be relied upon as a guide to either the place of origin or date, as many country woodworkers were equal in skill to their London counterparts. Indeed, the fact that large quantities of provincial antique furniture have survived in good condition is due, principally, to the high degree of craftsmanship involved. It is certainly no detriment to its merit for a piece to be labelled 'country made'.

The following chapters are primarily concerned with various styles and the general appearance of period furniture. But, before an attempt is made to assess the actual period, or even evaluate standards of craftsmanship of a particular piece, the article has already made its first appeal and has attracted attention by its purely visual aspect. Therefore it is necessary for the beginner to give some thought to the reasons for this initial appeal and to seek an answer to the, often puzzling question concerning the development of a keen eye which can, at first glance, suggest that an article is worthy of closer inspection.

It would be misleading to suggest that there is a quick and easy way to the attainment of expertise in the finer points of design assessment. In any subject of considerable complexity, intimate familiarity with the articles concerned is a primary necessity. This, however, is something which will be progressively achieved by anyone who is interested in period furniture. Good examples can be scrutinised in museums, galleries and antique shops; countless photographs of fine pieces can be studied in magazines and textbooks. Everything

Fig. 1. Example of good (*left*) and bad chair design

seen will contribute to the gradual composition of a clear mental picture of standard designs which can be applied to all future judgements.

To differentiate between good and downright bad design is comparatively easy, especially when furniture made after the conclusion of the Age of Oak is concerned. Standards of design were very highly developed in the eighteenth and nineteenth centuries, therefore students of styles can soon develop the ability to identify an article possessing merit. An exaggerated comparison is illustrated in Fig. 1, where a Hepplewhite-style chair (on the

Fig. 2. Over-embellishment of good basic design

left) is shown alongside a dreadful example loosely based on a similar design theme. Figure 2 shows how a perfectly correct basic design can be modified and over-embellished, to produce a tasteless article typical of the mid-nineteenth century at its worst.

The distinction between good and outstanding design is not so simply assessed. The differences are often subtle—obvious once they have been pointed out, but keen observation can be required in order to recognise them at a glance. They are to be found in pleasing, and therefore correct, proportions: in curves which flow easily, without sudden and disturbing changes of direction. In elegant tapering and the introduction of carefully considered curves, so slight as to be almost negligible. Little points, easily overlooked by a casual observer but providing the first indication of merit for the more discriminating student. A simple example is given in Fig. 3, where a chair-foot is shown with a plain, straight taper, and also with an added, slight curve providing a further degree of elegance.

The foregoing are the first features of which notice should be taken, prior to a closer and more detailed examination of craftsmanship and, finally, evidence of correct age. Subjects which are discussed in later chapters.

As styles and fashions of successive ages are studied, it is interesting to discern the emergence of clear patterns of development. The commencement can often be found in the early years of furni-

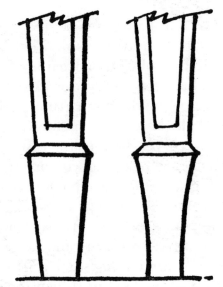

Fig. 3. Comparative examples of chair-feet

ture history, and the progression traced in logical stages to familiar articles in common usage today.

Typical examples of progressive design development can be seen in Figs. 4 and 5, which show the evolution of the writing-bureau and the chest-of-drawers.

Bible Box
c.1560

Writing Box
c.1590

Writing Box with Legs
c.1640

Writing Bureau
c.1700

Fig. 4. Evolution of the writing-bureau

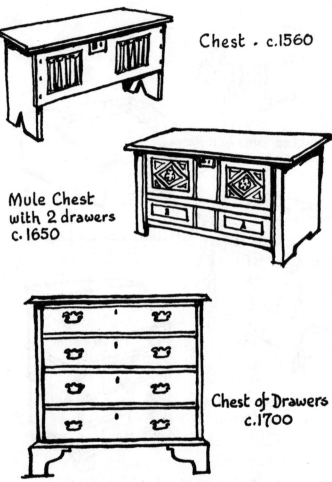

Chest · c.1560

Mule Chest
with 2 drawers
c.1650

Chest of Drawers
c.1700

Fig. 5. Evolution of the chest-of-drawers

1
THE AGE OF OAK
1500–1660

The gloomy influence of Puritanism which marred the closing years of the Oak Era, had probably been largely responsible for the present-day misconception which associates a dark, oppressive atmosphere with the furnishings of the Age of Oak. This idea is, in fact, wrong. Except during the later, cheerless years of Cromwellian dictatorship, decoration in the Middle Ages, and into the sixteenth and seventeenth centuries, was colourful in the extreme. The dark solidity of oak furniture and the drabness of stone walls was compensated, in ample measure, by lavish use of gaily coloured paint, and, in the more wealthy homes, rich fabrics. The woodwork of furniture itself was often painted—not always with taste, but with bright, cheerful colours. Some well-preserved examples of medieval furniture still bear traces of painted decoration and gilding. In prosperous houses wall-tapestries, embroideries and imported silks were used in profusion; the more ordinary homes depended upon correspondingly humble textiles—painted linen being a popular material.

Although the influence of the Renaissance in Italy filtered through to England and, undoubtedly, did much to enrich furniture design, its universal impact is frequently overestimated. The majority of craftsmen in this country received rather distorted, second-hand information regarding the Italian styles via Northern Europe. It is therefore reasonable to suppose that, as far as the design of domestic furniture was concerned, the English Renaissance could be attributed largely to an increasing awareness of decorative values, and also to progressive national development—the Italian influences taking the role of a powerful contributory stimulant. Some unadulterated Italian ornament did, however, embellish sixteenth-century English productions—particularly in London and the larger towns —due to the import of individual artists and craftsmen. The new styles were of considerable benefit to furniture-makers working close to the sources of design, but architects and sculptors were the principal beneficiaries, and it was a long time before the changes affected the work of rural craftsmen. Substantial advances in the arts of carving, inlay and panelling were the most important developments in furniture directly motivated by Renaissance influences.

The true Age of Oak actually dates from the twelfth century continuing until the close of the seventeenth. Furniture-making, however, did not develop as a specialist trade in England until about 1500; at which time the history of furniture becomes of interest to the student of styles, as well as to the social historian. Articles preserved from a prior date are rare indeed, and their design had no real influence on subsequent domestic articles.

Common homes in the Middle Ages and the early part of the sixteenth century were furnished simply, and it was only in the houses of the nobility and rich merchants that craftsman-made furniture appeared in general use. Crudely made tables, forms and stools—the latter often three-legged—were the usual items, and chests or coffers were widely utilised for the storage of anything of a valuable or perishable nature. In the poorer homes, the chest served as a seat or table. Although early examples are extremely rare, chests have survived in greater numbers than any other articles of furniture of this period.

The earliest form of carpenter-made chest was of 'archaic' construction comprising six boards only. Two side-pieces formed the legs, with the front and back boards crudely rebated into position and secured by nails. Very early examples were strengthened by iron strappings, and bent metal

Fig. 6. Plank or board chest of archaic construction,
c. 1560

staples formed hinges for the lid-board. Strap-hinges of iron were used on larger chests. This type of board, or plank, construction (Fig. 6) was used throughout the sixteenth century, towards the end of which joinery had become a more widely prac-tised craft. Early 'joined' pieces are distinguished by the use of dowel-pegs and the mortise-and-tenon joint. Framed construction, as used today, origi-nated some time about the close of the sixteenth century. In general, carved ornamentation of chests became progressively elaborate and finely executed. Gothic designs, composed of arches and interlacing, semicircular patterns, predominated until the introduction, from Europe, of the well-known linenfold style.

Prior to the sixteenth century, most dining tables in the larger houses were temporary structures of long boards laid upon two or three simple, sturdy trestles; thus the resultant large articles could be quickly dismantled at the conclusion of a meal. The master of the household usually had his own permanent, personal table of much smaller dimensions, against which the main board was abutted at right angles. This was also of trestle construction; the supports being made rigid by an oak rail, pegged into position (Fig. 7).

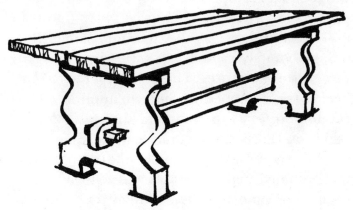

Fig. 7. Trestle table, *c.* 1490

In the early sixteenth century, the inconvenience of regular dismantling after every meal was alleviated by the welcome invention of the draw table. This method of construction enabled a permanent table, of moderate size, to remain in a set position, to be extended as required. This aid to space-saving has survived, almost unchanged in method of operation and is still in frequent usage. At the time of its invention it displayed a hitherto unknown degree of ingenuity, which heralded a progressive increase in the amount of thought devoted to convenience in the home.

Early draw tables were of plain, undecorated aspect, but increased elaboration followed in the form of carving and turning. The design of late Elizabethan examples has been perpetuated in the popular reproduction known today—probably quite erroneously—as the 'refectory' table. Bulbous, elaborately carved legs form the most easily recognisable feature. These incorporate a large 'melon-bulb', topped by an adaptation of a classical Ionic capital to complete the style correctly known as the 'cup and cover' leg (Fig. 8).

With the progression of the sixteenth century, increasing interest in comfort and convenience led to the development of less cumbersome articles of furniture. The trend was exemplified by the innovation of the gate-leg, or 'falling' table. This was produced in various sizes; larger patterns being suitable for dining and any general purpose. As another present-day survival of an old style, this practical design has remained unaltered apart from

Fig. 8. Elizabethan draw table, *c.* 1575

a few improvements in detail, for over three and a half centuries (Fig. 9).

Throughout the Middle Ages and well into the sixteenth century, seating was primitive and austere in the extreme, when adjudged by later stan-

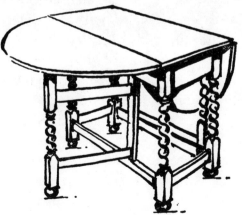

Fig. 9. Gate-leg or 'falling' table, *c.* 1640

dards of comfort. Until the seventeenth century, chairs were used only by the masters of larger households, being regarded as symbols of rank. Stools, forms and benches, very few original examples of which exist, provided the seating for ordinary people. The tripod stool was in general use from earliest times. Its pattern continued well into the Elizabethan Era, by which time joined stools and forms had become commonplace (Fig. 10.) Turned legs were not used for these articles until the late Tudor Period, and earlier joined

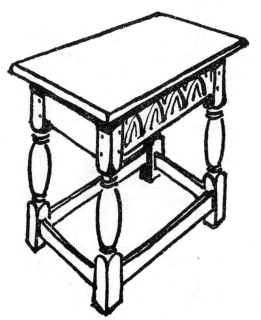

Fig. 10. Joined stool, *c*. 1540

stools were, virtually, miniature trestle tables with fixed supports.

The earliest known examples of bench seats, dating from the fifteenth century, consisted of plain planks mounted upon solid ends, Fig. 11. The under-frame was sometimes decorated with cut-out

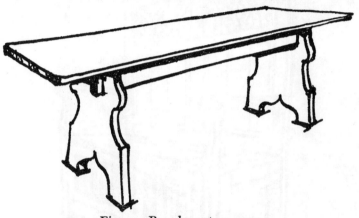

Fig. 11. Bench seat, *c.* 1500

Gothic pattern and fitted cushions were used as a rare concession to comfort.

The box-settle was a natural progression from the utilisation of the chest for seating purposes and was, basically, a simple chest to which arms and back-rest were added. Sizes varied considerably, ranging from box-chairs, seating one person to massive four- or five-seater settles. Seats were hinged at the rear in order to allow access to the enclosed space beneath (Fig. 12) Later examples dispensed with the lower, enclosed section and were made for the purpose of seating only.

Fig. 12. Box-settle, *c.* 1600

By the later years of Queen Elizabeth's reign, chairs were to be found in greater numbers in average dwellings—although they were not even then used by everyone. Usually heavy, ugly and uncomfortable, they were invariably decorated with

Fig. 13. Joined chair, c. 1600

an abundance of ornate carving and turnery (Fig. 13). Probably the only chair possessing any claim to elegance at this time, was the 'X'-frame, folding model; an early seventeenth-century adaptation of a very ancient pattern. This was the forerunner of upholstered chairs, in England, having a thick, fitted cushion supported by webbing, and a fabric-covered back-rest and arms (Fig. 14).

Upholstered furniture came into general use in the reign of James I, at the commencement

Fig. 14. 'X'-frame chair, *c.* 1600

of the seventeenth century. Chair seats and backs, and occasionally the arms, were padded, and covered with rich embroidery, tapestry or leather. Elaborate turning and fine carving characterise Jacobean dining chairs and stools, but the woodwork of upholstered items was usually quite plain (Fig. 15).

The 'Farthingale' chair (Fig. 16) is a particularly interesting example of the serious thought given, at this time, to purpose-design. Named after, and made to accommodate, the elaborate hooped dresses of the period, its seat was wider and higher than normal, and the low, padded back was given a generous rake.

An attractive little combination of table and chair, known today as the Monk's Bench, made its first appearance about 1600. It enjoyed considerable popularity in smaller homes, and provides one of the earliest examples of a 'novelty' item of furniture (Fig. 17).

The term 'cupboard' is nowadays applied to an

Fig. 15. Upholstered armchair, *c.* 1610

Fig. 16. Farthingale chair, *c.* 1620

enclosed container with doors. In medieval times, however, the word had a much more literal meaning, a cup-board being merely a supported, open shelf or ledge upon which cups or jugs could be placed.

The original rough, single board was developed, by domestic necessity into an acceptable piece of furniture, becoming a set of wide shelves supported by four sturdy, carved and turned pillars. This

Fig. 17. Table chair, *c.* 1600

familiar article was known as the court-cupboard; the prefix being of French derivation and meaning 'short' (Fig. 18).

The provision of doors, to provide enclosed containers, was a logical progression, thus later examples of the court-cupboard featured elaborately carved doors giving access to the enclosed space between the two upper shelves (Fig. 19). The cor-

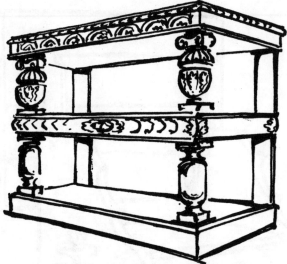

Fig. 18. Court-cupboard, *c.* 1580

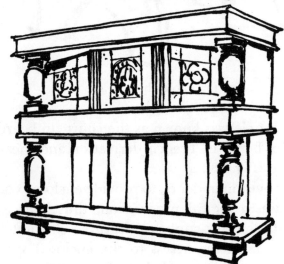

Fig. 19. Close cupboard, *c.* 1610

rect name for this piece of furniture is a 'close' cupboard.

Totally enclosed cupboards, with no open shelving, top or bottom, were called press-cupboards, or simply 'presses'—a name sometimes still used in Scotland. Many surviving, contemporary examples are similar in size and styling to the court-cupboard and close cupboard, except that the lower shelves are also enclosed, and fronted with carved doors. The upper doors were frequently recessed, and the two outer panels angled towards the rear (Fig. 20).

Fig. 20. Press cupboard, c. 1620

Lavishly carved ornament was featured on most larger pieces of furniture, as well as on chairs and stools. Many motifs and standard designs in common usage were particularly characteristic of the age, and a selection of these are illustrated in Fig. 21.

Smaller presses, or cupboards, were named in accordance with their various functions. Very small containers, usually with legs, were known as hutches, and were used during the sixteenth century in the poorer households for storing food. Somewhat bigger items of furniture, also used for the storage and distribution of perishable foodstuffs, were termed 'livery' or 'dole' cupboards (Fig. 22). Openwork doors, with carved tracery or turned spindles, provided the necessary ventilation, and such articles were often intended to hang on a wall; in which case, their size was rather less than that of the standing type with legs. Many surviving examples of wall cupboards have had legs added at a later date.

Credence cupboards and tables were used, in their domestic form, as adjuncts to the main dining table. Placed at the side of the room, they held the dishes to be tasted before serving to the master and his guests (Fig. 23). Originally the credence was an article of ecclesiastical furniture, which stood within the chancel rails, beside the altar, for the recep-

Guilloche

Grape & Vine Leaf

Strapwork

Gothic Arch

Linenfold

Lunette

Roundel

Thumb Carving

Romayne

Fig. 21. Examples of carved ornament in common use
during the Age of Oak

Fig. 22. Dole or livery cupboard, *c.* 1620

tion of the elements and vessels of Holy Communion.

The inclusion of drawers in pieces of furniture, although not unknown in the Middle Ages, did not become common practice much before the later part of the sixteenth century, when they began to be featured in the lower parts of chests. The useful composite result, known as a 'mule' chest (Fig. 24), eventually dispensed with the lidded section in favour of additional drawers. This became known as a chest-with-drawers, thus commencing the development of the popular article known today as the chest-of-drawers, or tallboy.

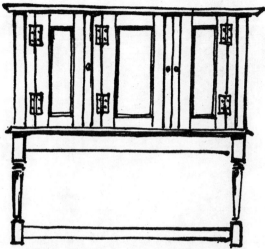

Fig. 23. Credence cupboard, *c.* 1600

A widely used and often indispensable article in the sixteenth and seventeenth centuries, was a lidded storage-box which has come to be known as a bible-box (Fig. 25). It is probable that bibles were sometimes housed therein, but these easily transportable containers were more generally used for the safe-keeping of miscellaneous articles of value. The lids of earlier boxes were flat, but, following the spread of literacy and consequent wider usage of books and writing materials, a sloped top with a lipped lower edge, transformed the simple storage-box into a rude form of desk (Fig. 26). Legs were added, at a later date, to commence the evolution of the writing-bureau.

Fig. 24. 'Mule' chest, *c*. 1650

Ornaments, as used today for purposes of visual embellishment only, scarcely existed during the greater span of the Age of Oak. Many decorative articles would be scattered about the rooms for specific domestic use, but their positioning would be expedient rather than consciously artistic. Pride of possession would doubtless encourage the dis-

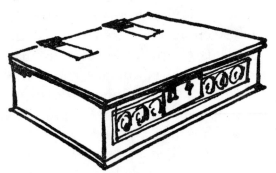

Fig. 25. Bible-box, *c*. 1560

Fig. 26. Bible, or writing-box, *c.* 1600

play, for instance, of a valuable imported tapestry, but, in the main, distribution of miscellaneous articles was functional. In the great halls, hanging banners and battle standards would doubtless add interest to the colourful scene, but their aesthetic contribution was incidental to their value as status symbols of the time.

After the formation of the Commonwealth in 1649, puritanical standards began to influence the design of furniture. Ornament which had become progressively elaborate, was regarded with stern disapproval by Cromwell and his followers. Craftsmanship suffered as design became severe and restrained but, although carving temporarily disappeared, turned ornament was acceptable to the austere eyes of the Puritans, and therefore flourished during the period of their influence.

One of the few attractive examples of the change of style retains some measure of popularity, even today, in the form of the Cromwellian dining chair. Solidly constructed, with turned legs and stretchers, the seats and backs of this practical chair design are covered with leather, secured with brass, dome-headed nails.

Tables and cupboards were likewise denuded of their decoration and embellishments, with the only desirable consequence of increased concentration on the achievement of pleasing proportions.

Although the oppression and miseries of Cromwellian puritanism did much to dampen artistic development in England, the traditional skill of the ordinary craftsman was fortunately unaffected, and the enforced period of restraint probably served to encourage the enthusiasm for improved design and lavish decoration which became released with the blossoming of the Restoration.

CHRONOLOGICAL TABLE
FOR THE AGE OF OAK

Richard III	1483–1485	Close of the Middle Ages
Henry VII	1485–1509	
Henry VIII	1509–1547	Import of Italian craftsmen
Edward VI	1547–1553	Early Tudor
Mary	1553–1554	Influence of Italian Renaissance
Phillip and Mary	1554–1558	
Elizabeth I	1558–1603	Late Tudor: Elizabethan
James I	1603–1625	Jacobean
Charles I	1625–1649	Carolean
Commonwealth	1649–1660	Cromwellian

2
THE AGE OF WALNUT
1660–1720

Following two decades of strife and oppression, the return from exile of Charles II heralded a dramatic change in the domestic scene. A spirited revival of culture, inaugurating in London and spreading enthusiastically throughout the country, was the natural outcome of the peoples' reaction to their release from austerity.

In the home, embellishment for the sale of appearance only, was no longer regarded with disfavour, thus the inventiveness of the designers and the skills of the craftsmen were liberated, and encouraged in full measure. Traditional skills were further stimulated by the influx of new, decorative furniture design from Holland and France. The English Court, having lived for many years in lavish European luxury, naturally returned from exile with grandiose ideas for improvement which were eagerly adopted by the comfort-starved British populace.

Effects of the Restoration had scarcely begun to achieve nationwide influence when trade was almost completely, albeit temporarily, halted by the outbreak of the Great Plague in 1665. However, a compensating initiative was provided soon afterwards. As London began to recover from the destruction caused by the catastrophic fire of 1666, furniture-making entered a period of reconstruction on a hitherto unknown scale.

The prior import of new continental design received unforeseen impetus, and manufacturers made energetic efforts to fulfil urgent needs with speed, elegance and elaboration.

Walnut had, by this time, superseded oak as the fashionable furnishing timber of the period. Lighter and more easily worked, its appearance and colour were considered to be in closer accord with the elegant styling contemporaneously in favour, and its texture was receptive to delicate and detailed carving. Oak was, of course, still much used, especially in country districts, and most chairmakers were discovering that beech was well-suited to their craft. The early part of the Age of Walnut was enriched by the appearance of many new, decorative woods—including lignum-vitae, ebony, olive and coromandel—which were imported to augment the English yew, holly, sycamore, laburnum and miscellaneous fruitwoods, in providing the materials for elaborate veneering and marquetry.

The technique of floral marquetry, although not unknown in previous years, did not develop to any great extent until later than 1670, at which time the work of Dutch craftsmen perfected and popularised this form of ornament.

Designed with an elegance much enhanced by continental influences, the quality of turned embellishment improved progressively throughout the period, and carved ornament became extremely elaborate. The immense degree of skill appurtenant to this age is exemplified by the outstanding artistry of Grinling Gibbons, master-carver to Charles II.

A considerable numerical increase in smaller articles of domestic furniture characterised both the early and later Walnut Periods. Tables with drawers, purpose tables, cabinets, writing-desks with minute drawers and pigeon-holes, firescreens and foot-stools, together with an endless variety of highly decorative luxury items such as elaborately carved frames for pictures and mirrors, candle-stands, and boxes for every conceivable purpose. Gilding and silvering became popular, and increasing use was made of metals, mother-of-pearl and tortoiseshell for marquetry and inlay. In fact, every material available was exploited in the search for new and novel embellishment.

Some of the most easily recognisable features of

the age are to be found in the shapes and styles of
supports. The cabriole leg made its first appearance
in England, and adaptations of European-turned
patterns became typical of the prevailing taste. The
older twist-turning, however, increased in popularity—to such an extent that many ill-equipped,
country makers hand-cut the 'barley-sugar' spirals,
without the aid of a lathe, in their efforts to meet
the demand. The finish of supports was improved
by the addition of shaped feet—many taking the
form of an animal paw or hoof. A later development was the 'ball-and-claw' foot, a design which
persisted throughout the whole of the succeeding
century.

Design and cabinet-making matured progressively and markedly throughout the Age of Walnut,
and the period can be clearly subdivided into
distinctive styles, Thus most pieces of furniture,
especially those of later years, are identified in
accordance with, and bear the name of, the
monarch reigning at the time of their manufacture.
The Restoration furnishings of Charles II and his
successor, James II, are invariably given the
general classification of 'Late Stuart'. 'William and
Mary' and 'Queen Anne' being names given to
styles of the final two decades of the Walnut
Period.

A typification of the outburst of ornament which

took place during the immediate post-Restoration years can be seen in the design of ordinary chairs. In dramatic contrast to Cromwellian severity, an abundance of carving was combined with twist-turning, and newly introduced, cane-weave back and seat panels completed the metamorphosis (Fig. 27). More expensive chairs were made of walnut, but beech—often darkened with black stain—was more commonly used. Country-made chairs did not usually carry such elaborate ornament (Fig. 28), although solid backs invariably featured the current trend for decorative carving.

Much oak was still used in the provinces, and baluster-turning symbolised the chair-making of rural craftsmen, especially in the North of England.

Matching chairs in flamboyance, foot-stools were lavishly carved, and often upholstered in velvet or tapestry with gay fringes and trimmings (Fig. 29). The fashionable cane-work was also used for seats; the crude, wide mesh of earlier examples becoming progressively refined.

The day-bed, following its introduction in Court circles, made a completely new innovation in England, and rapidly became popular in fashionable society. Styling of the raked back-rest was similar to that of contemporary chairs, and the framed base, covered with cane-mesh, was usually

Fig. 27. Charles II dining chair, *c.* 1670

supplemented by well-padded cushions. Very few day-beds of this period have survived, but evidence of their continued influence can be seen in the evolution of the couch and sofa.

The reactionary flamboyance of the earlier Walnut Period became somewhat restrained towards the close of the 1680s and the reign of William and Mary brought, to English furniture, the true

Fig. 28. Country-made chair, *c.* 1670

graciousness of design associated with the seventeenth and early eighteenth centuries.

Chair-backs retained their useful height, but the degree of carved ornament was diminished, the centre part often consisting of plain, solid splat with shaped edges. Top rails showed a tendency towards a hooped shape and, for the first time, the hitherto upright back became curved to fit the sitter. Drop-in, upholstered seats also first appeared about 1690 (Fig. 30).

Fig. 29. Examples of foot-stools

Techniques of upholstering developed rapidly towards the close of the seventeenth century and, by the time of Queen Anne's accession to the throne, many patterns of fully upholstered easy-chairs were in production. High-backed, with side wings and thickly padded arms and seats, they were usually covered in rich velvets, or fabrics decorated with fine needlework.

The cabriole legs of earlier wing-chairs were rather long and, although the shape of the legs

Fig. 30. Examples of dining chairs, c. 1700

themselves were elegant, they were unsuited to the added weight of construction and upholstery, thus necessitating the use of stretchers which were quite out of keeping with the leg-style. This fault was rectified in due course, when more sturdy legs which retained the cabriole shape, in stumpy form, were evolved. The different styles of wing-chairs are illustrated in Fig. 31.

The embellishments added to leg-endings, to which earlier reference has been made, was characteristic of the attention devoted to detail and finish by the designers of the William and Mary and Queen Anne Periods. Carved scroll-feet had been used previously, and the paw-foot was not new, but

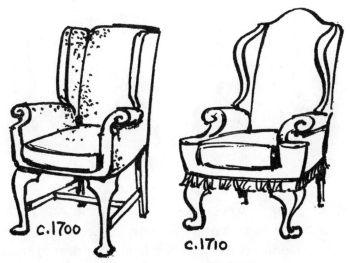

Fig. 31. Upholstered wing-chair, *c.* 1700
Upholstered wing-chair, *c.* 1710

the introduction—from France about 1700—of the
cabriole-leg, inspired new styles in the varying
degrees of elaboration; some of which continued
with but little modification, throughout the eighteenth century. Principal types of ornamental feet
are shown in Fig. 32.

Apart from the addition of embellishment, the
basic design of dining tables changed very little
during the years which followed the Restoration.
The gate-leg variety continued to enjoy its considerable popularity, with the addition of twist-
turning for legs and rails, and the old form of
heavy draw table remained in constant demand.

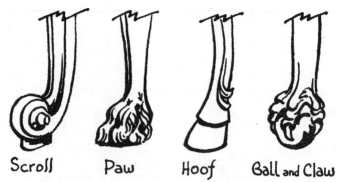

Scroll   Paw   Hoof   Ball and Claw

Fig. 32. Examples of ornamental feet

After 1680, however, elegance began to supersede solidity. Construction became lighter, legs less cumbersome and heavy stretchers disappeared with the increased utilisation of the cabriole leg for dining tables. As a consequence of the current vogue for small, highly decorative articles of furniture, the development of the side-table was rapid. Made for all imaginable purposes, many were attractively veneered and decorated with marquetry. Mouldings were added to previously square edges, and fashionable cross-banding improved the perimeter of many table-tops.

Drawers were featured in many purpose-made tables and, towards the end of the William and Mary Period, their construction became refined by the introduction of the stopped dove-tail joint. Fronts of many drawers were finely veneered, and edged with half-round moulding. Edge-mouldings with a slight frontal overlap were rarely used on drawers prior to the reign of George I. In addition to the new adaptations of earlier styles, table legs showed a marked Flemish influence, typified by 'mushroom' and 'inverted-cup' shapes, and later examples, whilst retaining basic profiles, easily

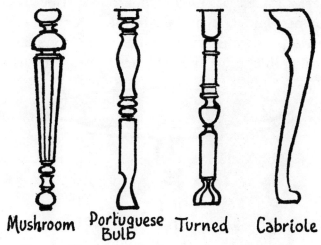

Mushroom   Portuguese   Turned   Cabriole
         Bulb

Fig. 33. Typical basic shapes of ornamental legs

outclassed their continental originals in refinement and shapeliness (Fig. 33).

As with all newly introduced furniture styles, country-makers developed their own, individual variations on currently fashionable designs. Many of these have survived, and although perfectly meritorious in their own right they can be regarded as being truly representative of the period only in the area of origin. An exception however, must be made in the case of the tripod table, which was made throughout the country in virtually unmodified form. This attractive design—a typical example of which is shown in Fig. 34 enjoyed universal and lasting popularity from the time of Charles I. Oak was used for its construction in the provinces and rural areas, but in London and other more sophisticated parts smaller walnut versions of considerable grace and elegance were made, to be

Fig. 34. Country-made tripod table, *c.* 1690

used as elevators for candle-stands, as well as for general purposes as 'occasional' tables.

Although constructionally unnecessary, a completely new type of decorative stretcher made its appearance, and soon became a characteristic feature of late seventeenth-century small tables and bureaux. A basic 'X' shape of flat section and curved profile joined all four legs close to the floor. The centre point of the 'X' was frequently surmounted by an ornamental finial (Fig. 35). This additional embellishment was also used for chairs and indeed, for any other articles of furniture with legs of length sufficient to display the feature to good advantage.

Fig. 35. William and Mary side-table, *c.* 1690

The development of the bureau and writing-desk provides one of the most spectacular advancements in domestic furniture of the later Restoration and Stuart times. The reign of Charles II saw considerable refinement of the bible-box-on-legs of the previous era, and the latter quarter of the seventeenth century produced writing-desks, bureaux, cabinets and bookcases in profusion. These ranged from small, boudoir pieces (Fig. 36), to large and imposing combinations of desk, chest-of-drawers and bookcase.

Increasing efficiency of nationwide postal services promoted the art of letter-writing into a fashionable habit, thus making a major contribution to the demand for writing-desks. Craftsmen and designers, seizing the opportunity to display skill and ingenuity, produced articles incorporating much intricate cabinet-making in the form of multiplicity of small drawers and pigeon-holes. Carefully contrived, secret compartments were often included in desks of all sizes.

Earlier writing-cabinets, called escritoires, consisted of a tall frame enclosing numerous drawers and compartments. This upper section, surmounted by a moulded pediment, was supported by four, five, sometimes six, legs of typical contemporary shape (Fig. 37). A large drop-front, covering the upper compartments served as a writing surface when open. The face of the drop-front, which was visible when closed, was often most beautifully decorated with marquetry. An alternative lac-

Fig. 36. Small desk with twist-turned legs, *c.* 1680

quered decoration, known as japanning also became very popular. Oriental designs in rich lacquers, liberally embellished with gold, provided a completely new flavour of magnificence. Boulle-work—an expensive marquetry of tortoiseshell and metals named after its French inventor—was featured on some of the rarer pieces.

The high drop-front of the escritoire certainly

Fig. 37. William and Mary escritoire, *c.* 1685

offered ample writing surface, but its inconvenient projection resulted in the development of a much improved design, which is still used today (Fig. 38).

Of moderate height, and mounted upon a set

of drawers, a 'writing-box' with a smaller, drop-hinged front, gave access to an arrangement of compartments and drawers which were recessed to allow an extra, flat surface within the carcase itself. Although a complete unit in itself, the small

Fig. 38. Small writing-desk, *c.* 1700

bureau was sometimes extended to become the base for an upper stage consisting of a double-door bookcase or display cabinet as shown in Fig. 39.

Large bureau-cabinets were amongst the most magnificent items to represent the Age of Walnut. They were invariably well-proportioned and taste-fully embellished. Traditional straight, moulded cornices did not lose their appeal but graceful,

Fig. 39. Walnut bureau-cabinet, *c.* 1705

curved pediments or architectural inspiration in the form of double or triple arches, were characteristic of these handsome pieces of furniture. The tall double doors were sometimes glazed, but panels of beautiful, plume-patterned veneer, or the lately introduced English mirror glass, were more typical of walnut examples.

The traditional storage chest, in varying degrees

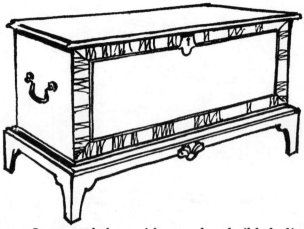

Fig. 40. Lacquered chest with carved and gilded plinth,
c. 1700

of elaboration remained in demand throughout the Age of Walnut; some expensive examples being highly decorative, with richly carved plinths and lacquered finish (Fig. 40). As a fashionable article of furniture, however, its popularity gradually declined in favour of the much more useful chest-of-drawers.

Many small sets of drawers were mounted upon stands, and all types of legs used for tables were regarded as being suitable supports. Some particularly attractive examples were made in the Queen Anne Period, when cabriole legs were in vogue (Fig. 41).

The tallboy, which consisted of two stages mounted on bun-feet, or a low plinth, found much

Fig. 41. Chest-of-drawers on stand, *c.* 1705

favour in its capacity as a generally useful article. Its purpose in the home was functional, rather than decorative, although many attractive variations were made, some reaching monumental size, with architecturally styled cornices and elaborate veneering (Fig. 42).

Although the tallboy enjoyed a long period of usefulness, a much lower single-stage chest of five drawers—three full width, and two small ones at

Fig. 42. Tallboy, *c.* 1705

the top—was found to be much more convenient, and gradually superseded the larger article in quantity production (Fig. 43).

Chests-of-drawers were often used as items of bedroom furniture, the smaller, more compact designs giving service as dressing-tables. These provided an alternative to the charming little three-

Fig. 43. Low chest-of-drawers, *c.* 1705

drawer tables specifically made for the purpose (Fig. 44).

Framed toilet-mirrors, hinged on to a stand and small enough to rest conveniently upon a dressing-table, appeared about 1680. The base of more expensive examples consisted of a casing enclosing several minute drawers, designed for safe-keeping of cosmetics and trinkets. This innovation gained immediate favour, sustained for over two hundred years (Fig. 45).

Fashionable combinations of carved ornament and lavish gilding involved the use of Gesso. All kinds of furniture, from small mirror-frames to elaborate console tables utilised this material. Bare

Fig. 44. Queen Anne Period dressing-table, *c.* 1710

wood did not provide a satisfactory base for gilding, therefore a ground of Gesso paste—a mixture of whiting and parchment size—was first applied to the surface requiring embellishment.

Sometimes the gesso paste was applied thickly, roughly modelled and, when set, itself relief-carved to the required design. Highlights were burnished, and finally treated with gold-leaf.

At the close of the seventeenth century, English taste in interior decoration had become very highly developed and, most important, the influence of professional designers was no longer confined to the homes of the wealthy.

Considerable refinement of architectural thought caused many smaller houses to be built

Fig. 45. Hinged toilet-mirror with drawers, *c.* 1710

with a view to gracious living and dignity of appearance, and this development was mirrored in the treatment of the interiors. The increasing prosperity of the country improved the purchasing ability of ordinary people, and their consequent enthusiasm for comfort and luxury was assuaged by a ready availability of beautiful furnishings, both home-produced and imported.

Rural furniture-makers continued, as in preceding ages, to produce their own hybrid styles, and better features of earlier design combined with free adaptations of newer fashions. Although sometimes less refined in proportion, when compared with London-made articles, much surviving provincial furniture is, nevertheless, pleasingly representative of the high standard of craftsmanship which prevailed, at the time, throughout England.

Although manufactured output was most prolific during the Age of Walnut, the nature of the wood itself rendered it less durable than either the oak of earlier times or the subsequently used mahogany In consequence, a large proportion of the contemporary production has perished and first-class specimens of seventeenth-century walnut furniture are, unfortunately, rare.

Some illustrations of various types of moulding and decorative motifs widely used at this time are included for purposes of reference at this stage (Figs. 46 and 47). Most of them were first introduced as embellishments of English furniture during the periods of Oak or Walnut, but their appeal continued, with the result that most continued to be used during the following Age of Mahogany and, indeed, throughout both the eighteenth and nineteenth centuries.

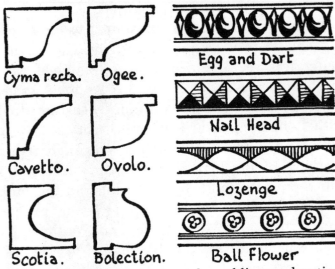

Fig. 46. Examples of ornamental mouldings and sections

Fig. 47. Examples of carved and applied ornamental motifs

CHRONOLOGICAL TABLE
FOR THE AGE OF WALNUT

Charles II	1660–1685	Restoration
James II	1685–1688	Late Stuart
William and Mary	1688–1694 ⎫	
William III	1694–1702 ⎭	William and Mary
Anne	1702–1714	Queen Anne

It should be noted that walnut remained in fashion after the accession to the throne of George I. Thus the first five years of the official Georgian era belong, as far as the history of furniture is concerned, to the Age of Walnut.

3

THE AGE OF MAHOGANY 1720–1805

The precise date marking the succession of mahogany as the fashionable timber of Georgian times is impossible to assess with complete accuracy. Designers and consumers were ready for a change of style in the eighteenth century and cabinet-makers found the crispness, close grain and rich colour of mahogany to be entirely adaptable to new fashions. The opportune demise of walnut was due, in no small measure, to a European shortage, which had become acute by 1720. A factor, further encouraging the choice of mahogany as a logical successor came in 1721, when an Act of Parliament removed much of the burden of import duty previously imposed. It can, therefore, be said that mahogany was firmly established as the principal furniture-maker's wood, well before the conclusion of the reign of George I, in 1727.

Several varieties of the new timber were used. In earlier years of the eighteenth century, Spanish mahogany, from the West Indies, was in great de-

mand, but this was soon surpassed in quantity usage by a Cuban variety: this was not only easier to
work but also possessed a much more decorative
grain. A further, lighter kind of mahogany from
Honduras—often known as baywood—was generally used in the solid for carcase construction;
Cuban veneers being employed for finishing.

More than any other period in the history of
furniture, the eighteenth century can be called,
with justification, the Age of the Designer. Previous
centuries had certainly produced designers of high
calibre; Inigo Jones (1573–1652) and Daniel Marot
of the Walnut Period being outstanding examples.
Their activities were confined, however, to Royal
Courts or great houses and their influence, though
undisputed, was scarcely felt by the ordinary people
of their lifetimes. In the Georgian Era, however,
the work of fine London craftsmen was no longer
the prerogative of the few, and the influence of their
published designs was able to permeate the whole
country.

The synonymity of the names Chippendale,
Hepplewhite and Sheraton with the Georgian era
is inescapable and, in order to survey the period
in true perspective, it is important to assess the
work of these designers in relation to the universally improved standards of the time.

Thomas Chippendale (1718–1799) was born in

Yorkshire and eventually became the senior part-
ner of a London cabinet-making concern, Chippendale and Haig; a firm of considerable repute, but
not outstanding distinction. Several firms existing
at the same time were superior in status and many
produced furniture of at least equal quality. Not-
able amongst these were Vile and Cobb—who enjoyed Royal patronage, a favour denied to Chippendale—Ince and Meyhew, Gillow of Lancaster and
William Hallett.

Chippendale was, however, an astute man of business and, in 1754, he compiled and published the
Gentleman and Cabinet-Makers Director, a catalogue of designs by himself and his employees.
This was virtually the first trade pattern-book, and
it is upon this publication and its subsequent en-
larged reprints, rather than outstanding merit as
a craftsman, that his legendary reputation was
founded.

The importance of the many pattern-books published in the mid-eighteenth century cannot be
overstressed. They were sold, in quantity, throughout the country, thus making new styles and designs
available to rural and provincial craftsmen very
soon after their innovation. Prior to this, years
could elapse before styles which were inaugurated
in London percolated through to furniture-makers
in remote areas. Thus, the 'time-lag' which had al-

ways existed between the introduction of a new design and its universal acceptance throughout the country, no longer existed.

Country craftsmen were able to work—within the limits of their skill and equipment—to the patterns of the leaders of fashion, and many pieces which survive today are classified as, for example, 'Country Chippendale'. Lacking, perhaps, the superb craftsmanship of the London maker and of proportions rather less elegant, they are, nevertheless, worthy specimens of good, eighteenth-century, English furniture-making.

In common with Chippendale, George Hepplewhite was also a North-countryman who, following an apprenticeship with Gillow of Lancaster, established his own business, in London, in 1760. Although undoubtedly a craftsman of outstanding skill, his workshop was modest and his reputation undistinguished prior to the posthumous publication, by his widow in 1788, of an important work of reference, the *Cabinet Maker and Upholsterer's Guide*. This comprehensive work contained a wealth of beautiful and well-tabulated material comprising an assemblage of contemporary styles. It made no claim to being a catalogue of original design, although its contents certainly included much of Hepplewhite's own work.

The lasting fame of Thomas Sheraton (1751–

1806) is based solely upon his published work as a designer and author. Although he possessed expert knowledge of cabinet-making and was able to write with practical authority, having spent several years as a trade apprentice, he never had a workshop of his own. His rather poor life was dedicated to the teaching of drawing, and the production of several written works dealing with most aspects of cabinet design.

The appearance of his most important work, the *Cabinet Maker and Upholsterer's Drawing Book*, published originally in four parts between 1791 and 1794, founded his unchallenged reputation as one of the great designers of the age. Featuring delicate construction, extreme elegance of line, and the use of satinwood, the 'Drawing Book' supplied patterns which, although lacking some of the grandiosity shown by earlier designers, found immediate favour and created the now famous 'Sheraton Style' which continued, with various adaptations, throughout the Regency and Victorian Periods.

It is important to note that specific styles of the Georgian Era are often identified by the name of the designer who originated the style. Therefore the appellation 'Chippendale or 'Hepplewhite' does not necessarily mean that the article concerned was actually made in their workshops. Indeed, this would be impossible in the case of Sheraton, who made no furniture at all. Therefore, unless old bills, receipts and record-books are available for purposes of authentication by proof of an original source of purchase, association with a 'master's hand' is almost impossible to ascertain. In most cases, although an article may be a splendidly made, accurate interpretation of a published design by a famous name, any of the better cabinet-makers of the period could have been responsible for its manufacture. Except in circumstances where its authenticity is indisputable, furniture is usually designated in more general terms; for example, 'Side-table, c.1760, in the style of Thos. Chippendale.'

Two architects motivated by the debatable theory that complete furnishing, as well as building design should be encompassed by the scope of their profession, made some particularly noteworthy contributions to the already considerable variety of Georgian interior decoration.

In the early part of the century, the creations of William Kent enjoyed a brief vogue. Intended to be in harmony with the revived Palladian style of architecture, of which he was a major exponent, these monumental productions were principally confined to the interiors of stately homes, and although historically interesting they did not greatly

influence ordinary furniture of his time. Nevertheless, they made for a radical change in design
theory, and therefore did influence later styles to a
considerable degree.

The Classical Revival, dating from the 1760s,
was largely inspired by the work of Robert Adam,
a distinguished architect, whose fastidious attention to detail helped to make his interiors into
models of academic taste. His beautifully designed
furniture possessed impeccable proportions, and
whilst bearing basic characteristics of contemporary
fashion was sufficiently individualised by the addition of classical ornament to become regarded as
a style in its own right. The influence of the Classical Revival was great indeed and inspired much
of the elegant furniture of the later years of the
eighteenth century.

The early Georgian Period was not distinguished
by any particularly marked change in chair design.
Palladian influences were mainly confined to the
residences of higher society, and much of the appearance associated with the late Walnut Period
persisted for some years. Although various new
styles were tried, they were mostly transient and
constituted the results of a haphazard pursuit of
originality, rather than exemplifications of a current trend.

In parts of the country, however, the Windsor

chair had begun to enjoy widespread popularity. Probably originating in Buckinghamshire, the design was produced with many local variations, each bearing characteristics identifiable with their counties of manufacture. A solid, shaped seat was common to all, and although any convenient wood was used, beech and elm predominated (Fig. 48). A hitherto unused shape, the hoop-back, became particularly favoured for smaller chairs (Fig. 49).

A pierced centre splat was introduced into later chair-backs; the ornament of which was often copied, in simplified form, from more sophisticated

Fig. 48. Typical Windsor chair (comb-back),
mid-eighteenth century

Fig. 49. Windsor chair (hoop-back), mid-eighteenth
century

furniture (Fig. 50). The ladder-back chair became
popular during the first half of the eighteenth
century, particularly in the North of England. A
ladder-back is also illustrated in Fig. 50.

During the latter half of the eighteenth century,
excessive ornament, in the Baroque manner, lost
much of its previous appeal, although Chippendale
continued to make use of restrained variations in
many of his productions. In consequence of his
acute sensitivity to changes in fashion, his designs
showed characteristics which clearly reflected the
vagaries of prevailing taste. None were exaggerated,

Wheel-Back • Spindle-Back • Ladder-Back

Fig. 50. Examples of country chair-backs

Rococo   Ribbon-back   Gothic

Fig. 51. Examples of typical Chippendale-style chair-backs

however, nor were they in any degree eccentric, as exemplified in the successive styles of his chair-backs (Fig. 51).

The cabriole legs of Chippendale chairs were more shapely than many produced in earlier years, and the improved profile was terminated by a ball-and-claw foot on many expensive examples. Decorative carving in the form of acanthus foliage, or a cabochon-and-leaf motif, frequently adorned the knee of the cabriole shape. Straight legs of square section, chamfered and fluted, were much in vogue at a later date.

Upholstered chairs of all sizes, and in every degree of opulence, were in increasing demand, but the examples made in Chippendale's workshops were generally modestly dimensioned and upholstered, and of a square, rather squat appearance (Fig. 52).

Fig. 52. Chippendale-style upholstered armchair, *c.* 1760

The introduction, by Robert Adam, of a lighter style combining Classical and French derivatives, had considerable bearing upon chair designs of the period (Fig. 53). Although the very high cost of Adam-designed furniture precluded its appearance

Fig. 53. Adam oval-back chair with embroidered seat and back

in other than the richer households, the influence of extremely elegant style did permeate, with advantage, most of the better-class contemporary workshops.

The combination of grace and practicability to be found in the finest Georgian chair design, is typified by the artistry of George Hepplewhite, whose original and distinctive patterns are reproduced, in faithful detail to this present day (Fig. 54).

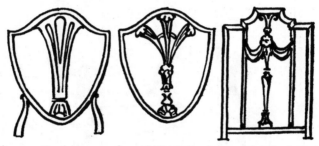

Fig. 54. Basic examples of Hepplewhite-style chair-backs

Chairs illustrated in Thomas Sheraton's drawing-book provided a radical change from earlier productions of the Georgian Era (Fig. 55). Their limbs were refined to a stage of delicacy which bordered upon fragility. Carving was no longer favoured to any extent. Inlay, in straight lines, became the usual alternative decoration; the technique being known as stringing. The cabriole shape disappeared completely, to be replaced by a square-sectioned leg with, in most instances, a distinctive taper. Later examples featured taper turning, often with reeded, or cabled, decoration.

Ornamental feet were no longer advocated, a rather plain peg-foot being the most common replacement. The majority of Sheraton chair-backs were roughly square in outline, and horizontal splats eventually superseded the traditional vertical type.

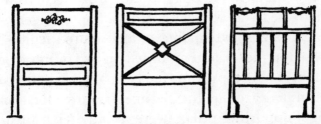

Fig. 55. Examples of typical Sheraton-style chair-backs

Although the demand for settees had become considerable, and examples were included amongst the wares produced by most furniture-makers, this particular item was almost completely neglected by Sheraton. Nor were stools of any kind featured in his published designs.

The well-known, and still most popular fabric designs, collectively known as 'Regency Stripes' began to be favoured for seat coverings about this time; the pattern being admirably suited to combination with the angular aspect of the frames.

One of the most popular items now particularly associated with the Georgian style of furnishing, is the pedestal dining table (Fig. 56). This extremely elegant and practical piece of furniture did not, in actual fact, become widely used until the latter part of the eighteenth century, when it became popularised by Sheraton and, to a somewhat lesser degree, Hepplewhite.

The full-sized pedestal table was developed from the earlier tripod design, and progressed from a single-pedestal type with drop-sides, to larger, sectional tables, extendable to any desired length by loose top-pieces, and mounted on two or more pedestals. Table-tops were finely veneered, and often decorated around the perimeter with cross-banding. Supporting pillars were usually taper-turned, with added fluting or reeding, the more expensive examples being finished with ornamental brass toes.

Fig. 56. Pedestal dining table, *c.* 1790

Pier Tables, specifically made to stand against the pier between windows, became a decorative necessity in many Georgian houses. An example of one style is illustrated in Fig. 57, but they were made in divers sizes and patterns—although of a more or less uniform height. The shape of the top usually formed a shallow rectangle or half oval, sometimes decorated with veneer or marquetry.

Console—or bracket—tables were often of very ornamental aspect. Made to stand against, or be affixed to, a wall, their single support consisted of an extravagantly decorated bracket; especially flamboyant examples of which took the form of an eagle carved from solid wood and fully gilded. Outstretched wings acted as supports for the top, which was sometimes made of marble.

The 'Pembroke' design was suitable for either medium or small-sized general-purpose tables (Fig. 58). The useful drop-leaf had, of course, been utilised for many years, but attained its highest degree of popularity towards the conclusion of the eighteenth century. The top was occasionally—especially in the case of smaller pieces—decorated with marquetry, and the two flaps rested upon hinged brackets when raised. A small drawer was included at one end only; a matching dummy drawer-front gave decorative uniformity to the other.

The enormous demand for occasional tables in

Fig. 57. Pier table, *c.* 1785

later Georgian times was engendered, to a great extent, by the widespread social habit of entertaining to tea. Tripod tables were produced in appropriate sizes, especially for this function; many of the designs being of much elegance. Perimeters of table-tops were usually lipped to prevent accidental sliding-off and consequent breakage of china, and, on the better articles, the lip was scalloped, to form what is known as a 'pie-crust' top. As an alternative to the lip, a gilded metal gallery of about 1 inch in height was sometimes provided. Most tea-tables of this shape were provided with a hinge which al-

Fig. 58. Sheraton-style Pembroke table, *c.* 1795

lowed the top to be folded into a vertical position, as a space-saving expedient.

Smaller tables, including scaled-down replicas of ordinary tripods were designed for the purpose of placing beside the chairs of individual guests, and the still popular nest-of-tables was introduced at this time, with a similar use in view.

A useful appendage to the practical furnishings of the dining-room appropriately known as a 'dumb-waiter', originated during the first half of the century, to become of increasing service in most middle-class homes. Many of these articles were attractively proportioned and beautifully made, averaging about 4 feet in height, with three circular, revolving tiers of vertically diminishing diameter (Fig. 59).

Some of the finest cabinet-making of the eighteenth century is to be found in examples of the library, or drum, table (Fig. 60). These beautiful articles consisted of a tripod pedestal, supporting a circular top-section of depth sufficient to accommodate several drawers. The drawer-fronts and their surrounding fascias were veneered, and table-tops covered in gilt-embossed leather. The majority

Fig. 59. Dumb-waiter, *c.* 1760

Fig. 60. Drum or library table, *c.* 1795

were between 3 and 4 feet in diameter—although many smaller examples are in existence.

The idea of a comprehensive item of furniture, designed to hold all the miscellaneous impedimenta of the dining-room was originally conceived by Robert Adam. In previous schemes, a large side-table was flanked by matching pedestal cupboards, on which stood a pair of receptacles, for cutlery and water, in the shape of ornamental urns. This cumbersome grouping was collated by Adam into a single piece of furniture, monumental in appearance in early examples but becoming progressively refined (Fig. 61).

Lighter sideboards, of very much more grace-ful proportions, were developed by Hepplewhite and Sheraton; the serpentine and bow-front shapes have since become synonymous with their names, and typify their sensitive approach to practical design problems (Fig. 62).

Fig. 61. Adam-style sideboard, *c.* 1770

Carcases of longer sideboards were supported by six legs; four in front and two at the rear. Wide, shallow drawer—or a single drawer—occupied the centre section, with either a deep, square drawer, or a cupboard, on each side. Fine inlay and stringing decorated the front and legs. Drawer-fronts provided an ideal surface for the display of figured satinwood veneers. Serpentine and bow-fronts were most common, but on some examples the flow of the serpentine curve was interrupted to give a flat,

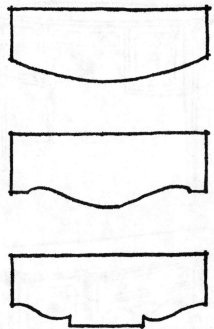

Fig. 62. Plans showing shapes of late-Georgian sideboards

slightly projecting centre section. The resultant variation was known as a 'break-front'. Illustrations of typical sideboards are shown in (Fig. 63).

The legs of the majority of London-made sideboards were slender, tapered, square in section and, as mentioned previously, decorated with stringing. In later designs, however, Sheraton favoured taper-turning embellished with fine reeding. Brass ring drawer-pulls were generally used, in conjunction with stamped back-plates, and orna-

Fig. 63. Sheraton sideboards. *Above*: Bow-front.
Below: Break-front

mental back-plate rails of brass were featured on some larger Sheraton pieces.

As in former times, country craftsmen were naturally influenced by fashionable trends and,

aided to an increasing extent by the availability of
new pattern-books, produced much fine furniture
in all the current styles. Their wares, however, continued to cater for local tastes and requirements,
and noteworthy amongst such products is the kitchen article of lasting esteem, which has come to be
classified under the general title of 'Welsh dresser'
(Fig. 64). In actual fact, these practical and handsome items were made in many different districts;
Lancashire and Yorkshire dressers being particularly distinctive and frequently larger than those
made in Wales itself. Invariably made of oak, kitchen dressers were sturdily constructed in two

Fig. 64. Examples of kitchen dressers mid-eighteenth
century

stages, the lower part consisting of a set of drawers and cupboards or drawers alone, mounted on turned legs or stumpy feet. This was surmounted by a framework of open shelving to hold a display of plates and jugs.

Designs of most early Georgian bookcases were based on the styles of their walnut predecessors, but the monolithic, classical creations of William Kent and other Palladian Revivalists, brought a change of appearance which became refined into tasteful elegance by Chippendale and Robert Adam, in the mid-eighteenth century. Angular broken-pediments (Fig. 65), replaced the curved arches of the Queen Anne Period, and were often 'supported' by fluted pilasters, capped with Ionic, Doric or Corinthian capitals. The 'swan-necked' pediment, although originating about 1720, was much favoured by Chippendale and retained its popularity well into the Victorian Age (Fig. 66).

Several alternatives to the sloping drop-front appeared on bureaux towards the close of the eight-

Fig. 65. 'Broken' pediment

Fig. 66. 'Swan-necked' pediment

eenth century. A type known as the Secretaire presented the appearance of a deep top drawer when closed but, when pulled outwards, the front hinged forward to provide a flat writing area (Fig. 67). An upward-rolling, rigid cylinder-front was briefly popular—and was again made in Victorian times—but it became exceeded in esteem by its derivative, the Tambour or roll-front. This latter form of flexible, slatted shutter was favoured by Sheraton for use, in particular, on smaller ladies' desks (Fig. 68).

Flat-topped, pedestal desks were not unknown in the previous century but it did not attain any widespread favour until about 1750. Most were oblong in shape, although some expensive specimens took an oval or kidney contour. Being frequently large and heavy articles, pedestal-desks were made in three separate parts, the top section locating on to the already positioned pedestals (Fig. 69).

A particularly beautiful piece of furniture made its first appearance at the end of the eighteenth century. Of delicate construction and elegant

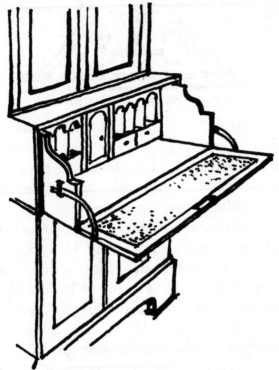

Fig. 67. 'Secretaire'-type desk front

styling, the Carlton House writing-table enjoyed well-deserved, fashionable esteem, and continued to be made in considerable numbers well into the nineteenth century (Fig. 70).

Most chests-of-drawers were made with the traditional straight front until approximately 1745, when fronts of serpentine shape, which had been in vogue in France for some years, became fashionable

Fig. 68. Tambour-top desk

Fig. 69. Pedestal desk, *c.* 1795

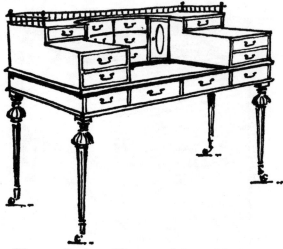

Fig. 70. Carlton House writing-table, *c.* 1805

in England. Many were richly decorated with carving, marquetry and a gilt bronze embellishment known as ormolu. Shaped doors, covering the drawers, offered an admirable base for elaborate floral marquetry. These newly-styled combinations of usefulness and ornament were generally known as commodes (Fig. 71).

Although many of his designs featured straight fronts, Sheraton was particularly associated with the bow-shape. His ornamentation, however, was considerably restrained when compared with many contemporary examples of the commode (Fig. 72).

The popularity of the rather cumbersome tallboy declined towards the end of the century, al-

Fig. 71. Chippendale-style commode, *c.* 1760

though they continued to be regarded as useful in larger homes. Most examples followed, in general, the pattern of the smaller chests, both straight and bow-fronted.

Corner-cupboards, which originated during the Age of Walnut, did not become really popular until after the reign of George I. Throughout the remainder of the eighteenth century they were manu-

Fig. 72. Bow-front chest-of-drawers, *c.* 1790

factured in quantity; oak being the material principally used for their construction in provincial
areas. Mahogany was used for finer pieces, and
many beautiful examples have survived, although
these are comparatively rare. Two types were
made, one being a single-stage cupboard, often
mounted on a stand with legs; and the other a two-
tier design which occupied the whole corner from
the floor to a height of 6 feet or more. In the case
of the latter article, the doors of the upper tier
were frequently glazed.

Smaller articles of domestic convenience were
invented and manufactured in abundance during
the late Georgian times. Thomas Sheraton, in par-

ticular, devoted a great deal of his inventive skill and ingenuity in this direction. Articles designed specifically for the bedchamber have survived in considerable quantities which, although often displaying exquisite craftsmanship, usually possess quaintness rather than beauty when adjudged by modern standards. Sheraton washstands, especially those designed for corner standing, are good examples of Georgian purpose design (Fig. 73),

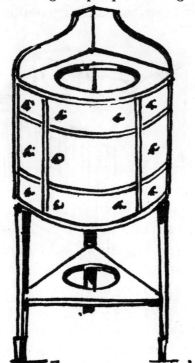

Fig. 73. Sheraton corner washstand

and a great deal of thought was expended upon the styling of pot-cupboards, in order to impart an air of delicacy to a purely functional article (Fig. 74).

Decorative firescreens became essential items in most Georgian withdrawing-rooms, many being extremely attractive articles of fine craftsmanship and decoration. In the constant search for novelty, however, some rather odd and not very practical designs were evolved; examples like the Sheraton firescreen-cum-writing-table becoming quite popu-

Fig. 74. Sheraton pot-cupboard with Tambour front

lar. Some of the most elegant styling for this type of article was to be seen in the tripod firescreens, consisted of an oval or shield-shaped panel—often decorated with embroidery—mounted on a graceful, turned pillar, terminating in tripod feet.

Knife-boxes, tea-caddies, jewel-caskets and work-boxes all received the attentions of the most skilled designers of the period, consequently surviving items of this kind can provide the collector with extremely desirable examples of the beauties of eighteenth-century design and craftsmanship.

CHRONOLOGICAL TABLE
FOR THE AGE OF MAHOGANY

George I	1714–1727	Palladian Revival
George II	1727–1760	
George III	1760–1820	Classical Revival

N.B. The Regency Period officially commenced in 1811, but in the history of furnishing it is accepted that the Age of Mahogany ends in 1800.

4

THE REGENCY PERIOD
1805-1830

Applied to interior furnishing, the term 'Regency' is merely a title of convenience. It does not imply accurate chronological coincidence with the actual Regency of George, Prince of Wales, which commenced in 1811 and continued until 1820. Signs of a changing style were apparent by the end of the eighteenth century, and although the manner of furnishing associated with the period did not come into common usage until about 1810 it is generally accepted that, as far as furniture is concerned, the Regency Period extends over the first thirty years of the nineteenth century.

In basic principle the completely different fashions, which achieved immediate acclaim, stemmed from the contemporary French Empire style, the mixed inspiration of which was derived from ancient Roman, Greek and Egyptian ornament and architecture. Adaptations produced in this country are, in fact, sometimes given the name of 'English Empire'.

The extensive spread of the new French style was engendered by the publication, in 1807, of *Household Furniture and Interior Decoration,* a book of designs by an architect, Thomas Hope, an enthusiastic devotee of Classical and Empire decoration. Hope's name has become synonymous with the Regency style. This was followed, in 1808, by a well-illustrated *Collection of Designs for Household Furniture and Interior Decoration* by George Smith. A prominent cabinet-maker of the time. Smith made his own adaptations of antique styles which, if sometimes imaginative and not always of true academic correctitude, nevertheless served to excite wide public interest.

The popularity of mahogany continued; but satinwood, which had become favoured at the latter end of the eighteenth century, was largely replaced by rosewood. Amboyna, zebra-wood and maple were also favourites of the Regency cabinet-makers.

Metal—usually brass or ormolu—embellishment, both applied and inlaid, was used extensively, and Boulle-work enjoyed a brief revival about 1815.

Wood marquetry was no longer in vogue and had almost completely disappeared from furniture by the turn of the century. It was, however, to make spasmodic reappearances throughout the nineteenth century.

The problem of combining the ornamental attributes of metal and wood was not tastefully solved by all contemporary craftsmen, with the result that the decoration of much Regency furniture was somewhat ill-proportioned and overdone. The better work, however, possessed a graceful clarity of form, much enhanced by the addition of hitherto unexploited motifs in cast and inlaid brass. Inlaid borders, lattice-work, galleries, lion-mask handles and cast paw-feet were typical embellishments, and more expensive pieces incorporated heavy gilt castings representing the sphinx, griffin, winged lion or Theban monster. Human heads were also featured, often attached to a winged animal body. The classical lyre was much used as a motif, and as a shape for supports.

A revival of Chinese influence occurred during the mid-Regency period culminating in an outbreak of pseudo-orientalism which was represented, in its ultimate form, by the Royal Pavilion and its extravagant interior furnishings, which the Prince Regent caused to be erected at Brighton.

The constant quest for novelty, eccentricity and affectation lent a certain confusion to the emergence of original styles. Designers spared no effort to produce outstandingly different pieces of furniture, but the development of a characteristic, national style was delayed by their excessive devotion to conjecture concerning hypothetical treatment of nineteenth-century furniture by the ancient Greeks, Romans and Egyptians.

Much interesting furniture, of fine quality, was produced between 1800 and 1830, but although the great traditions of the previous century were continued to a considerable extent some deterioration was undoubtedly evident in standards of craftsmanship. This was partially a natural outcome of the economic state of the country, but a more probable, major causative was to be found in the increased use of newly available woodworking machinery.

It is interesting to note that the process of French polishing was introduced into England about 1815. The improved method of finishing was immediately, and universally, accepted and much furniture which had survived from the Georgian, and earlier, ages was stripped and repolished by the new technique.

Many chairs continued to be made after 1800 in the styles introduced by Hepplewhite, Sheraton and other designers of the preceding century, but the variety was soon supplemented by a new concept, a major feature of which has come to be regarded as one of the most familiar characterisations of Regency furnishing—the scroll. A typical scroll armchair is illustrated in (Fig. 75). Although the scrolled arms were placed too high for real comfort, these chairs were usually of most graceful proportions; the legs were given a scimitar-like curve, and the back-rail a scroll in miniature. Elaborate and expensive variations were made, which incorporated cast-metal rests for the arms, brass stringing, inlay, reeding and carving. Thomas Hope was responsible for the design of many outstanding, surviving examples.

Stools, with cane or upholstered seats, enjoyed

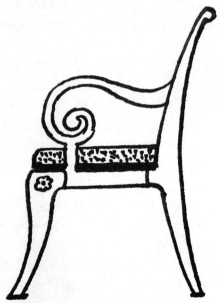

Fig. 75. Scroll armchair, c. 1805

a marked increase in popularity. The more simple and practical patterns served as music or dressing stools, but many were too elaborate to be used for any purpose other than that of pure decoration. Variations of the traditional 'X'-frame were common, and many extant specimens are lavishly enriched with scroll-work, ormolu, painting and gilding.

Regency flamboyance was exhibited in fullest measure in the varied designs of sofas, and every ornamental carving, painting and general embellishment of these often astonishing—and sometimes supremely elegant—creations. Heavily padded settees were temporarily outmoded in the early nineteenth century, the more classically inspired type of reclining couch being favoured for the withdrawing-room. Angular shapes were not unusual, but scrolled forms with asymmetrical ends were much in vogue (Fig. 76). The embodiment of an armrest within the ornament of the back, was a feature of many couches and sofas.

Very few changes of a major nature occurred in the design of dining tables during the early years of the Regency. The pillar-and-claw style was mostly favoured for smaller tables; four claws, instead of the usual three were often used after 1800. Tripod tables in the manner of Hepplewhite and Sheraton retained their earlier popularity.

Fig. 76. Regency reclining-couch, *c.* 1820

Circular tops for dining tables became fashion-able about 1805. The instability of early, larger examples being corrected by the addition of four supplementary ballusters. These, and the main single pillar support, were mounted on a platform which was, in turn, supported by claw feet at each corner (Fig. 77).

Fig. 77. Circular dining table, *c.* 1815

Massive, solid supports were often used, even for comparatively small tables. Usually of highly ornamental aspect, these excessively robust bases invariably took the form of free adaptations of classical architecture. The complete article was named, pompously and in keeping with its ponderous appearance, a monopodium (Fig. 78).

One of the favourite and most pleasing articles of furniture in common use during the early nineteenth century, was the small sofa-table (Fig. 79). Derived from the Pembroke style of Georgian times, these stylish and useful articles were made of

Fig. 78. Marble-topped monopodium in the style of Thomas Hope, *c.* 1807

mahogany, satinwood or rosewood, relatively undecorated, and usually about 5 feet in length—
with the flaps raised—by about 2 feet in width.
Used for general purposes in most homes, the sofa-
table was so named on account of its original function as a ladies' table, intended to stand in front of
a sofa.

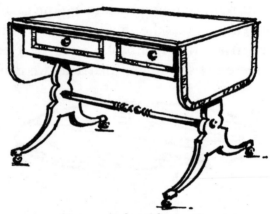

Fig. 79. Sofa-table, *c.* 1805

Mid-Regency years brought a return to favour
of large, pedestal type sideboards, with matching
knife-boxes standing on each side-pedestal. The
general aspect of most patterns was not quite so
monumental as that which characterised the
William Kent designs of the previous century, and
the impression of solidity was lessened by the introduction of a vertical taper to the pedestals. The

knife-boxes, although free-standing, were intended
as an integral part of the design, and were usually
given a matching, tapered profile. On later pieces,
brass plate-rails gave way to solid back-boards
with progressively elaborate carving which, although alien to the delicacy of much Regency
styling, possessed a heavy grandiosity which fore-
shadowed impending Victorian fashions (Fig. 80).

Most larger bookcases followed the basic characteristics of the late Georgian Period, with the addition of some reasonably restrained, gilded metal

Fig. 80. Pedestal sideboard, *c.* 1825

embellishments and brass inlay. A distinguishing Regency feature was introduced in the form of gilt, metal lattice-work for door panels; this was backed by pleated silk of delicate colour.

Much ingenuity was used in the design of small bookcases and stands. These typically Regency items have survived in considerable numbers to become desirable collectors' pieces of outstanding merit. Mahogany and satinwood were the materials principally used with the addition of rosewood, which became progressively popular for drawing-room furniture of all kinds. Illustrations of two typical miniature pieces representative of the period are shown in (Fig. 81).

The popularity of small pieces of furniture was not confined to bookcases. Innumerable varieties of miniature work-tables, writing-bureaux, dwarf cabinets, cupboards, dumb-waiters and screens were manufactured in profusion. A great number have survived to become some of the most eagerly sought specimens of later antique furniture. Some were, quite naturally, adaptations of earlier designs, to which currently fashionable embellishments were added. It is sometimes difficult to distinguish between late Georgian and Regency pieces—but many of the latter were original conceptions bearing features of identification unmistakably nineteenth century in origin. For example, lyre-shaped

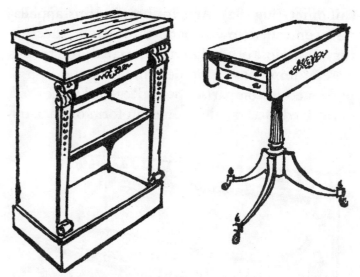

Fig. 81. Examples of miniature furniture, c. 1820:
Bookcase and work-table

supports, latticed brass-work and stands with four claw-feet instead of three.

A considerable selection of completely new items of small furniture appeared during the first thirty years of the nineteenth century, many being note-worthy only by virtue of their appeal as novelties. Several innovations, however, possessed much dainty charm, which gained for them immediate and lasting favour.

In the forefront of articles in greatest demand was the compact and useful composition of cup-board, drawers and display shelves, known as the chiffonier (Fig. 82). Articles bearing this appellation continued to be made throughout the century, but most of the later Victoriana productions were of unprepossessing design, heavy and ill-proportioned in comparison with Regency pieces.

Evolved as a strictly utilitarian form of 'rack-on-

Fig. 82. Chiffonier, *c.* 1820

legs' for holding plates and cutlery in the dining-room, the Canterbury became a very popular general-purpose article used in many homes. In more recent times, the name is much more familiarly associated with a later function as a sectioned holder for sheet-music.

Another domestic piece, regarded with great affection throughout Regency and Victorian times, was the teapoy (Fig. 83). Until its innovation

Fig. 83. Teapoy, *c.* 1830

about 1810, small tea-chests—or 'caddies' as they came to be called—stood on any convenient table; the teapoy, however, was designed as a complete standing unit, the tea-chest itself being supported by a single decorative slat, or a pillar and four claws. Later examples became most ornamental, often decorated with lavish brass inlay or marquetry.

The variety of ladies' writing and work-tables was unending (Fig. 84). The former were invariably decorative rather than practical, the emphasis upon daintiness rendering them almost fragile. In contrast, the beautifully made and elegant work-tables and sewing-boxes were made with full consideration for their principal function (Fig. 85).

By comparison with the earlier periods, the duration of the Regency was short and the era produced furniture which was the least typically English of all. Although considerable claim to artistic distinction is unquestionable, a very little contribution to the development of truly English style was evident. Most of the features now regarded as being synonymous with the period, were accurate plagiarisms or adaptations of contemporary French fashion, which was, as already described, derived, in turn, from the styles of ancient Greece, Rome and Egypt.

Many of the most attractive Regency pieces

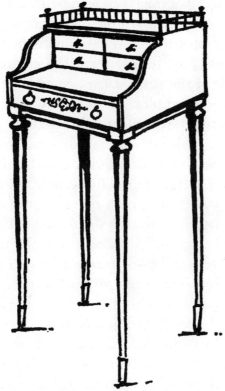

Fig. 84. Ladies' writing-desk, *c.* 1820

were, however, happy combinations of the designs of the preceding mahogany period with the imported styles, and it is fortunate that the tendency towards an excess of sophistication did not succeed in diluting the traditionalism and insularity of most small, country craftsmen.

Although the French-inspired vogue was mainly

transient, some of the influences persisted well into Victorian times, finally losing identity in the haphazard intermixture of styles which characterised the furniture of the mid-nineteenth century. With the ending of the Regency, a demand for opulent appearance at low cost, plus an escalating search for change and novelty, caused most British manufacturers to subjugate their traditional instincts of taste and elegance, with the result that furniture design, in England, entered the worst phase of its history.

Fig. 85. Ladies' work-table, *c.* 1830

5

THE VICTORIAN PERIOD 1830-1901

Strictly speaking, Victorian furniture has no place in a historical survey, as articles made after 1830 are not officially regarded as being 'antique'. With the passing of the years, however, some flexibility must be given to the date-line and, despite the serious deterioration in standards of taste and craftsmanship which marred much of the production of the time, many articles of furniture possessing undoubted merit and interest were made, and indeed, retain an artistic charm sufficient to render them worth inclusion in any present-day home.

During the first twenty years of Queen Victoria's reign, there was little to interest the student of design, and the chaotic, cumulative effect of haphazard tastelessness reached its ostentatious climax with the Great Exhibition of 1851. This flamboyant explosion of an indiscriminate and speculative quest for grandeur seemed to impart a steadying effect upon designers and manufacturers, with the result that evidence of a more co-ordinated approach became manifest almost immediately.

The universal public demand for an outward show of opulence, however, remained unabated, and this naturally led to camouflaging of cheap, inferior constructions by means of a superfluity of embellishment—an unfortunate commercial practice which was to survive.

Although craftsmanship continued to deteriorate for nearly a decade following the Great Exhibition, efforts were eventually made to re-establish some semblance of taste into furniture design. The multifarious permutations of pseudo-classical, mock-oriental, Neo-Gothic and past English styles which swamped the domestic scene, reached an ultimate stage of commercialism by about 1860, at which time the first signs of more clearly defined design began to emerge from the morass. No really strong resurgence of good taste was immediately evident, but sincere efforts were made by several prominent designers to guide prevailing fashions into more refined channels. The results were accepted eagerly into the insatiable market for something different and novel.

A mid-century revival of the Gothic taste, and its subsequent exploitation, benefited the architecture of the period, and interiors of public buildings, rather than the design of furniture. Exponents of the style, in particular A. W. N. Pugin and William Burges, devoted much attention to furniture, but their approach was too architectural to be wholly successful in the smaller, domestic field. A widespread public interest in antique furnishings accompanied the Gothic revival, with the result that a considerable quantity of English and European reproductions appeared on the market. Many of these were well-made, creditable articles but, unfortunately, manufacturers were unable to resist the temptation to make minor, but nevertheless undesirable, alterations to the original designs. Extraneous embellishments were often added, thus many basically good reproductions degenerated into mere hybrids.

Various attempts to break away from the popular, fussy interpretations of traditionalism were made in later years, with a resultant evolution of a cleaner, more simple style. Under the general designation of 'Art Furniture', lines became more severe, and a greater degree of concentration was given to improved construction and the creation of a definite order. The movement was greatly influenced by the activities of an artist and designer, William Morris, who founded a company which specialised in the production of superior, handmade domestic furniture. Simplicity of line, and a rather studied emphasis on honesty of construction characterised the early output of the firm, and the somewhat massive appearance of many productions in no way detracted from the carefully considered, graceful proportions.

About 1880 the Morris company originated, and produced, in large quantities, cheap bedroom furniture of tasteful design usually stained a dark green colour. The demand for this entirely new conception was great, and resulted in the style being freely adopted by other manufacturers—together with the popular, rush-seated 'country' chairs which represented a later Morris innovation.

The revival, by prominent manufacturers, of older country styles, greatly stimulated the advancement of the Arts and Crafts Movement which swept the country during the last decade of the century to influence, not only the appearance and construction of manufactured furniture but also the tastes of the general public. The foundation of the movement consisted of a collaboration between craft guilds and associations which had been inspired by strong reaction against current deteriorations of standards. The range of domestic and other articles produced under its auspices was wide indeed, and emphasis was always placed, primarily, upon careful craftsmanship and a balanced style modelled on that of the eighteenth century. Some good furniture was produced at this time, including first-class reproductions of Period pieces. The majority of contemporary designs however, can be judged today, only by individual reaction to their appearance. They must, at least, be respected for their comparative sincerity.

Immediately prior to the close of the century, styles became again confused. The appropriately named 'Quaint style' produced some very odd adornments for the, already overcrowded, Victorian homes. Typical examples being monstrous corner-pieces, and huge settles with high carved backs incorporating gaudy, leaded-light panels.

A French import, the Art Nouveau Movement, made a brief appearance which only served to add to the existing confusion. The style was certainly original, and may have possessed some merit in its country of origin. Its manifestation in England was, however, somewhat clouded by intermixture with local fashions of equally bizarre character.

Although the memory of vulgarian taste and chaotic design is difficult to erase, the fact that comfortable well-made and sometimes beautiful articles were produced in the nineteenth century cannot be disputed. It is indeed unfortunate that their merit tends to be overshadowed by the preponderance of cheap commercialism and poor workmanship existing during the greater part of the Victorian Era.

The Victorians' love of comfort was typified by the lavishly stuffed, upholstered furniture of the period. Leather, velours and wool-fabrics, covering generous padding, contributed to the general air of opulence so beloved by all classes. Ornamental trimmings, braids and fringes added further embellishment. Upholstered furniture was made in every possible variation of shape and size, but two distinctive contemporary items—the Chesterfield and the Ottoman—deserved especial mention as they were not only typical products of the age but also continued to be manufactured, in modified forms, well into the twentieth century.

When first introduced, in early Victorian times, the ottoman was merely a low chest, covered all over with padded fabric: the top being cushioned to provide a kind of small divan. Later examples became more ambitious fully-upholstered, multiple seats of angular or totally circular shape, with low, centre or back-rests.

The Chesterfield (Fig. 86), enjoyed more lasting favour as a simple attractive design easily adaptable to changing tastes. Early examples of this low-backed settee tended to be of over-generous proportions, but provided a very high standard of comfort.

Many varieties of wooden chair produced during the nineteenth century, survive in quantity as

Fig. 86. Early Victorian Chesterfield

worthy examples of practical Victorian design at its best. The most familiar is the balloon-back chair (Fig. 87), which, in sundry degrees of elaboration, enjoyed universal favour from about 1835. Made of mahogany, walnut, rosewood or beech stained to simulate the more expensive woods, the frames were sometimes lightly carved, with turned or, in the case of drawing-room chairs, cabriole legs. A larger mutation, without arms, but possessing a fully upholstered seat and back—often covered in wool-tapestry—was known as a spoon-back chair (Fig. 88).

Windsor chairs of the previous century retained their popularity, the basic design continuing un-

Pre.1840•Note shape of backs•Post 1840

Fig. 87. Balloon-back chairs, *c.* 1840 (*left*), and later design

changed, apart from some minor details, until variants bearing but few of the characteristics of the originals were produced during the time of the Arts and Crafts movement. The first noteworthy developments were, however, produced as early as 1830: most widely favoured and lasting the Bow-Windsor and the Scroll-back (Figs. 89 and 90). The latter is classed as a Windsor chair, even though its simple shape is far removed from the familiar, traditional design.

The circular loo-table, originally named after a popular card-game, proved to possess general appeal, thus becoming a familiar piece, found in

Fig. 88. Spoon-back chair, mid-nineteenth century

the majority of homes (Fig. 91). The bases of large loo-tables were often sumptuously carved and inlaid decoration of the top was not uncommon.

The design of large tables, sideboards, cupboards and, indeed, all major articles of furniture produced in Victorian times, was of too heterogeneous a nature to allow isolated trends to be regarded as representative of the age. Many smaller articles, however, possess sufficient distinction and artistry

Fig. 89. Bow-Windsor chair, *c.* 1850

to impart a positive identity, associable with the period. It is also natural that, despite the confusion of styles and preponderance of fussiness, many attractive results should reward the great amount of thought and ingenuity expended on design and ornament.

In addition to the more obvious necessities, certain pieces of furniture came to be regarded as essential items for inclusion in most Victorian drawing-rooms. For instance, the importance given to the piano encouraged the manufacture of highly

Fig. 90. Scroll-back Windsor chair, *c.* 1860

ornamental music-stools, and a contemporary taste for assemblages of small knick-knacks provoked the universal usage of a handy set of tiered shelves, the name of which has become humourously synonymous with Victorianism—the whatnot (Fig. 92).

A delightful example of the ingenuity displayed in the provision of original items of miniaturised

Fig. 91. Loo-table, c. 1860

furniture, was the small desk known as a Davenport (Fig. 108). Produced in quantity during the
latter half of the century, this invariably finely-
made article contained plenty of drawer and storage
space, within very compact overall dimensions.
Although of solid, masculine aspect, it was regarded as a popular ladies' piece.

The most intriguing, from the point of view of
the modest collector, and frequently most skill-
fully made articles, were to be found amongst the
enormous output of secondary pieces, with which
the Victorians filled their rooms. Small occasional
tables for all purposes, ladies' work-tables and
boxes, miniature bureaux, firescreens, book-
stands, tea-caddies and plant-stands are but a few
of the infinite variety made, and embellished with

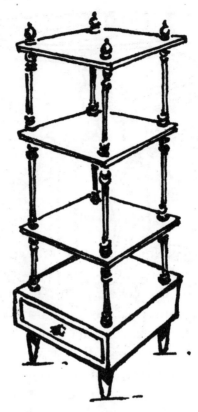

Fig. 92. A whatnot, *c.* 1865

every conceivable form of ornament. A great number were, of course, cheaply made and completely lacking in any artistic merit, but many have survived which displayed skilled craftsmanship and a praiseworthy measure of charm and elegance.

Fig. 93. Davenport, *c.* 1865

6

AUTHENTICATION OF ANTIQUE FURNITURE

The preceding chapters have dealt with basic styles, shapes, materials and ornament of the various periods. All these features are, however, applicable to genuine old furniture and also to good quality reproductions. A knowledge of styles is certainly a basic requirement for the student of period furniture, but ability to assess age, from evidence other than an authentic appearance, is no less important.

Finely made reproductions should, of course, never be despised. However great one's enthusiasm for the past may be, it cannot be denied that, from a purely visual angle, a really good nineteenth; or even twentieth, century piece can be a most desirable possession. This is especially applicable to copies made, perhaps, a hundred years ago therefore old enough to have acquired a 'patina' of age in their own right. Nevertheless, it is essential for the enthusiast or collector to know of the features which can assist an accurate authentication of any items which may be encountered.

One primary fact should be realised from the start. No mystique is involved. There are no vague, intuitive feelings, possessed by connoisseurs alone, which can identify an antique, or spot a fake, without the expert being able to explain his certainty. Indications are always present, for anyone to see, which suggest in a tangible way whether or not the piece is genuine.

An expert, accustomed to handling antiques regularly, notices small features automatically and may be almost unaware of their impact on his mind, but it is not intuition that causes him to authenticate, or suspect, a piece—just keen and practised observation.

'Patina' is a term frequently used by expert and amateur alike during inspection of a piece of old furniture. It refers to the distinctive, glossy surface texture built-up on the surface of wood over a period of many years. The depth and general appearance of true patina can be achieved only gradually and naturally by wear and usage, slight atmospheric erosion, light abrasions, waxing and constant polishing. It is therefore subtly different to a surface which has been given a rapid and recent gloss.

Although patina is an important factor in the assessment of Period furniture, the beginner is advised to regard it as a feature contributing to the attractiveness of a piece, rather than something from which age can be deduced, at least, until some experience has been gained by comparing the appearance of many articles of varying ages.

Probably the most certain method of detecting a reproduction, is to look for signs of staining. Not staining of the immediately visible surfaces, but the inaccessible, or under, parts of the piece concerned. For instance, the underside of a chair or table, drawer-linings, insides and backs of cupboards.

A genuine eighteenth-century, or earlier, piece of furniture should show no sign of stain whatever on these parts. Discoloration by dirt or age will certainly be visible, but it will be on bare wood, free of any artificial colouring.

Reproductions or copies must, of necessity, be artificially coloured by staining in order to impart the desired impression of age. It should be remembered that antiques were originally sold as new items, therefore deliberate efforts to achieve a bogus aged appearance were unnecessary.

Stain is also found to be used, often quite crudely, suggesting long usage on frontal and visible surfaces. Applied thickly, it is allowed to half dry, at which stage patches are wiped off to expose near-bare wood in places where signs of wear would be expected. Highlights of carved and turned ornament, chair-rails and arms, front edges of cupboards and similar articles are obvious places, receptive to this kind of treatment. The method of age-simulation was particularly popular in the early part of this century.

Deliberate maltreatment of a newly made piece of furniture, by blows from hammers and chains and severe abrasion, is known by a most descriptive term—'distressing'. Intended to produce a spurious effect of wear and tear, the process is frequently carelessly executed and overdone, therefore its detection is, very largely, a matter of pure observation only.

Even during a period of several hundred years, it is hardly likely that a piece of domestic furniture would receive dozens of severe hammer blows, therefore any quantity of deep, round-edged indentations found on any one item can be regarded with suspicion.

Within the scope of distressing comes the practice of rounding originally square edges with a spokeshave. Frequently, this will have been done to an exaggerated degree, resulting in an excess of roundness which would not have occurred in the process of normal usage. A thoughtless mistake, providing an obvious clue for the observant, is often made by the faker using the spokeshave on parts which would not be subjected to any heavy wear. For example, the back stretchers of chairs,

Obviously, there are many ways of distressing a piece of furniture by bruising, scraping, scratching, gouging and beating with blunt instruments. In practically all cases, detection is possible by application of logical observation.

When appraising an eighteenth-century chair, an expert immediately turns it upside down for a quick inspection of the underside. Evidence of staining is sought, as previously explained, but several other features can also provide important clues to suggest authenticity, or otherwise. No one of these is, by itself, conclusive but, all being indicative of the period can strongly suggest a genuine article.

The first point to be noted comes with the act of actually lifting the chair, namely its weight. A good, eighteenth-century chair would be made of Cuban mahogany; a solid, heavy wood. On the other hand, a reproduction of nineteenth-century, or later, origin would probably be lighter in weight as it would more likely be made from a lighter timber—Honduras mahogany or baywood.

In the case of dining chairs made in sets, frames were often numbered during the setting-out. Numbers were usually incised, with a gouge or small chisel, on the inside face of the back seat-rail.

During the eighteenth century, Roman numerals were invariably used.

It is always advisable to check the width of the armchair, or chairs, in a dining set. The practice of adding arms to single chairs in order to make-up a small set is not uncommon. Usually this is done skilfully by expert craftsmen and is, therefore, not immediately evident. The width of the front seat-rail should be measured, as that of the armchair should be 2 inches wider than the single. In the event of the armchair being a 'made-up' specimen, the two measurements will be identical.

Carved embellishment of mahogany furniture should be carefully examined. As a general rule, eighteen-century carving, executed in Cuban mahogany, is crisper and more decisive in detail than that found on the products of the following century. Shallow, rather 'woolly' toolwork is usually indicative of Victorian craftsmanship.

Although by no means an infallible rule, the lighter the colour of mahogany, the more likely a later date of origin. Cuban timber, in addition to possessing greater physical weight, tended to be darker in colour than the Honduras variety used later. Any mahogany presenting an orange appearance can, in practically all cases, be assigned to the Victorian period.

Detection of repairs to pieces of furniture of any period is, once again, largely a matter of keen observation. Clumsy repairs present no difficulty, as discrepancies between standards of craftsmanship will be immediately obvious. Much restoration, however, is executed with considerable skill and taste; new wood being carefully chosen and 'matched-in' by accurate staining and polishing. The presence of repairs naturally reduces the value of an article considerably, so the slightest lack of uniformity in colour, figuring or texture justifies meticulous scrutiny to ensure that the piece has not, at some time, suffered damage and subsequent restoration.

Valuable indications of correct age can be seen in the construction of drawers. Dates of the various innovations and changes can, of course, only be given as an approximation. It should be noted that changes, especially in earlier times, did not happen suddenly or universally. Often a considerable period elapsed between the innovation of an improvement, or new fashion, and its general acceptance throughout the country.

Drawer sides can provide a fairly reliable guide. In the case of good quality furniture, the thicker the side-piece, the older the article. The thickness rule is also applicable to veneer. Early hand-cut veneers being very much thicker than those used in the later part of the eighteenth, and the nineteenth century.

Drawer front-to-side jointing altered noticeably about 1680–1690 with the introduction and universal adoption of the 'stopped dovetail' as illustrated in Fig. 94. The practice of strengthening drawer-joints with nails ceased at this time; the improved joint was found to provide adequate rigidity.

Concerning the drawer-bottom; in the event of the grain running from side-to-side, a date after approximately 1730 can be assumed with reasonable confidence. Earlier examples were made with front-to-back direction of grain.

The insides of many drawers are finished by the addition of a quarter-round moulding which fits into the angle formed by sides, front and bottom. Mouldings were never fitted in this position by eighteenth century cabinet-makers, therefore an article possessing the feature can be given a post-1800 date of origin.

Until the use of nut-and-bolt fastenings became universal practice, about 1750, drawer-handles were attached by means of split-pins. This necessitated holes drilled right through the drawer-front. Later, more decorative handles are often added to replace original specimens, but, although back-plates cover the holes on the front, evidence of a

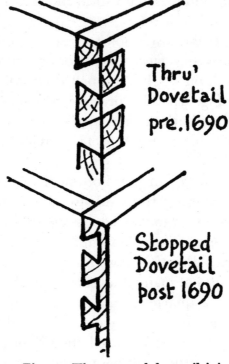

Thru' Dovetail pre.1690

Stopped Dovetail post 1690

Fig. 94. The stopped-dovetail joint

different type, or size, of handle can sometimes be discerned on the inside, proving existing handles to be non-original.

Drop or loop-handles were usual until approximately 1685, at which date 'D'-shaped handles with back-plates appeared. Most back-plates were solid at first, but pierced designs became common, and progressively elaborate, in the eighteenth century.

Circular and oval plates, stamped out of thin, sheet brass made their first appearance about 1795. Brass, lion-mask handles are associated with early nineteenth century and Regency styles.

7

WOODS

Identification of woods used in furniture construction and embellishment throughout the ages can be difficult at times. Common timbers can be so treated and polished that the more easily recognised features become lost. Photographs and written descriptions can help the aspirant to expertise only insomuch as they provide theoretical knowledge. The only way to achieve the ability to make immediate recognition is to create every opportunity to examine as many actual specimens as possible.

The beginner should never be diffident about asking the name of a wood which is unfamiliar, or about which some puzzlement may be experienced. Many people hesitate to make what they imagine to be a very elementary query, thus losing a chance to acquire a most valuable piece of knowledge for future reference. It is a fact that quite knowledgeable enthusiasts can often disagree over a point of timber identification, so a question concerning this, or any other feature in the field of antiques, is seldom likely to constitute the feared exposition of ignorance.

The remainder of this chapter is devoted to brief, descriptive details of woods likely to be encountered in a study of furniture. These may serve as a preliminary introduction to an essential aspect of identification.

AMBOYNA: Introduced into England in the mid-eighteenth century from the West Indies. Light brown with 'bird's-eye' figure. Always used as veneer, particularly in 1780–1820 period.

APPLE: Native fruitwood. Light brown with pinkish tinge; hard and close-grained. Usually used for inlay and veneer, although small items such as clock-cases were made of this wood in the late seventeenth century. Susceptible to woodworm.

ASH: Whitish wood with well-marked yellow-brown grain. Very tough and heavy. Generally used in the making of country furniture.

BEECH: Light brown with light, speckled grain. Distinctive darker flecks of medullary rays. Fairly soft and perishable. Used extensively since seventeenth century, particularly for chair-making and carcase work.

BIRCH: Light in colour and weight. The grain is not prominent but often possesses a rippling effect resembling Satinwood. It was used as a cheaper substitute for the latter timber in the late eighteenth century. Popular with rural craftsmen.

BOXWOOD: Very pale whitish-yellow. Very hard wood with no figuring. Used from the seventeenth century for marquetry and inlay work only.

CEDAR: First used in England in the seventeenth century. Light brownish-red with a grain similar to that of mahogany, for which it can sometimes be mistaken. It is, however, very much lighter in weight and was used only for drawer-lining, insides of cupboards and poor-quality furniture.

CHERRY: English fruitwood with particularly attractive golden-brown colour. Well-marked, straight grain. Used principally by country furniture-makers in the seventeenth and eighteenth centuries, and more widely for inlay and turnery.

CHESTNUT: Two main varieties have been widely used throughout the history of English furniture-making. Common, or Horse, chestnut is whitish-brown; sweet chestnut possesses a more red tinge. Both varieties are light in weight but durable, with strong, straight, indented grain. Apart from the lack of fleck markings of medullary rays, chestnut can be easily mistaken for oak.

COROMANDEL: First imported from India in the late eighteenth century. Striking black-and-yellow striped appearance. A popular veneer particularly useful for cross-banding.

DEAL: Also, correctly, called Scots Pine. Reddish in colour, with well-defined, straight grain. Used for carcase work and cheap furniture, from the mid-eighteenth century. Prior to this date, yellow pine of a similar nature was used.

EBONY: Imported from the East Indies. Known in England from medieval times. Used principally as an inlay and, more occasionally, for turnery. Very fine clock-cases were made in ebony from the late seventeenth century. A very heavy, close-grained wood of near-black aspect. Much so-called 'ebony' is in fact pear or other native fruitwood, stained black.

ELM: Medium brown in colour. Strong grain, in broad, slightly jagged bands. Owing to its susceptibility to woodworm and a tendency towards severe warping, few early elm pieces have survived, although the wood was in common usage from early times. Used for chests and seats of almost all Windsor chairs.

HAREWOOD: The name 'Harewood is given to sycamore which has been stained a grey-green colour. Used for veneering and marquetry of high quality in Georgian and Regency times. It enjoyed a brief revival of favour in the early twentieth century.

HOLLY: Very white, hard wood; similar in appearance to boxwood. Used for inlay, marquetry and, at the end of the eighteenth century, for stringing.

KINGWOOD: Introduced into England in the seventeenth century from Brazil. Lightish, warm brown in colour. Regular patterned figuring similar in formation to that of rosewood, but without the characteristic blackish markings of the latter.

LABURNUM: Distinctive, contrasting markings of dark brown and yellow make laburnum one of the most decorative of woods used, from the seventeenth century, for veneer work. Popular and most effective for 'oyster' style veneering.

LIME: Not used for furniture making or embellishment. Pale whitish-yellow, light in weight and close grained. The grain being exceptionally even and free from knots, makes lime a perfect wood for the carver. This was the material used by Grinling Gibbons and other great carvers of the seventeenth and early eighteenth centuries.

MAHOGANY: Became generally used for the making of furniture in England about 1720. For almost the whole of the eighteenth century, a heavy, close-grained timber of rich, deep reddish-brown colour was imported from the West Indies—San Domingo, Cuba, Puerto Rico and Jamaica. The term 'Spanish' mahogany is often applied today.

From about 1780, Honduras mahogany, or baywood, became used progressively. A very much lighter wood both in weight and colour; the latter being a golden-brown. Figuring is attractive and varied, containing many burrs and curls.

MAPLE: Although not unknown in England as early as the seventeenth century, it did not become popular until after 1800. A light yellow wood from the American Sugar Maple tree, the distinctive 'bird's eye' markings made a considerable appeal in Victorian times.

OAK: Strong, hard, heavy and durable. Honey-brown colour. Straight grain with prominent medullary rays which often stand slightly proud of the surface. Used for most good furniture before 1660. Thereafter restricted to country-made pieces and carcase construction.

PEAR: Pale, warm yellow or reddish-brown. Inconspicuous figuring. Liable to attack by woodworm. Used mainly by country makers, carvers or for inlay.

PINE: *See* Deal.

ROSEWOOD: A hard, heavy timber imported from Brazil and India. Rich colour ranging from hazel to reddish-brown with almost black markings. Liable to fade to a walnut colour in strong light. Very popular during Regency and Victorian Periods.

SATINWOOD: Two varieties became fashionable during the last twenty-five years of the eighteenth century, each possessing noticeably different characteristics. West Indian satinwood was used at first, to be succeeded, about 1785, by an East Indian wood. Both are pale golden-yellow, with straight grain and rich, light-catching figuring. The later satinwood, which fell from favour about 1800 after considerable exploitation by Thomas Sheraton, was heavier, of closer grain and lacked the brilliance of the West Indian variety.

SYCAMORE: Native wood of pale, yellowish-tan colour. Delicate, attractive grain formation with mottled figuring. Not very heavy, but hard and durable. Used since the Middle Ages for marquetry in the seventeenth century and as a popular veneer during the Georgian period.

TULIP WOOD: A close-grained, heavy wood of medium reddish-brown colour. Strong, straight grain made tulip wood well-suited for use in decorative veneering. First used in quantity in the mid-eighteenth century, often for cross-banding.

WALNUT: Both principal types of walnut—Regia (ordinary English) and Nigra (black walnut)— were grown in quantity in England by 1650. Both are rich, golden-brown in colour, with strong, clear, darker markings. From the latter quarter of the seventeenth century until the succession of mahogany as the fashionable furniture timber about 1720, much walnut used in this country was imported from Europe and Virginia. Widely used in the solid and for decorative veneering. Burr walnut veneers, cut from the base of the tree where the grain is turbulent and curly, were particularly valued. Very prone to damage by woodworm.

YEW: A hard, tight-grained, reddish-brown timber. Used for small, country-made furniture from an early date. Burr veneers used in the late seventeenth and eighteenth centuries for more sophisticated, good-quality furniture.

ZEBRA-WOOD: Imported from Guiana in the latter part of the eighteenth century. Mid-brown colour with close, striking stripes of near-black. Similar to coromandel, but rather more yellow. Employed only as a decorative veneer.

INDEX